The Boy With The Walrus Mustache

The Boy With The Walrus Mustache

By Zachary A. Schaefer

&

Illustrated by Elizabeth Gearhart

Dedication

To Kizzy and Claudia, for giving me the courage to complete this project and for having the confidence to pursue a life filled with passion, love, curiosity, and happiness.

There once was a boy named Benjamin who was born with a walrus mustache.

He was scared to make friends because of his looks.

So he spent most of his time buried in books.

Benjamin found things that he could do alone. Reading, writing, and playing the saxophone.

Benjamin loved learning ideas and writing songs,
But he had no one to share them with...
Until Claudia came along.

Claudia's curiosity and confidence gave her social grace,

But Benjamin was shy and embarrassed of his face.

Claudia didn't mind.
She thought it was neat.
Benjamin's mustache
was as big as her feet!

So she taught Benjamin to be proud of who he was.
That walrus mustache of his created quite a buzz.

The townsfolk wanted to meet this mustached boy.
He had something unique they all could enjoy.

With Claudia by his side,
she grasped his hand and went to town with pride.

Once the people saw his well trimmed hair, they also heard his music in the air.

Benjamin read the crowd his stories
and played songs he had written.
He was amazed at all the smiles and cheers he was gettin'.

Claudia helped Benjamin move beyond his shy approach...

And he became one of the town's most popular folks.

The End